CHANGE THE WAY YOU SEE YOU

I0382091

To:
_____

From:
_____

Date:
_____

Pretty Girl

CHANGE THE WAY YOU SEE YOU

STARR COBURN

CHANGE THE WAY YOU SEE YOU

Pretty Girl: Change the Way You See You
Copyright 2020 by Starr Coburn

Published by:

starrelitepublishing@gmail.com

All rights reserved. Pretty Girl: Change the Way You See You is copyright protected. No part of this book may be used or reproduced in any manner whatsoever without written permission except in the case of brief quotations embodied in critical articles and reviews.

ISBN: 978-17332183-1-3

ACKNOWLEDGMENTS

To Him who is the head of my life.

DEDICATION

To all the Pretty Girls around the world.

Change the way you see you

Dear Pretty Girl,

You are beautiful and wonderfully made. Life has not been easy for you, I'm sorry. You encountered scars that hindered you from loving yourself unconditionally. The scars forced you to push people away. You were afraid if they seen your scars, they would not love you.

Often you felt alone and later developed a huge void. The void you felt in your life caused you to look for love in all the wrong places. You settled for fabricated love. It was temporary and made you feel you were on a cloud, but left you in a state of despair.

Your scars reminded you of the tragic event that occurred, but it is also a reminder of how I kept you. You loved them unconditional. Sometimes you loved them more than you loved yourself. Instead of loving you back they left. I want you to know that they did not leave because you were not good enough. They left because they were not good enough for you. If I had not removed them from your life, you would not have known that you could live without them. I allowed you to fall so you know that I will always be there to pick you up. Despite the things you have gone through, you are doing great. Don't give up.

Sincerely yours,
Your Heavenly Father

CONTENTS

THE UGLY TRUTH...1
WATCH WHAT YOU SAY...2
WHO ARE YOU?..4
WHY SHOULD I FORGIVE HER?...8
BROKEN...12
SOME TRUTH ABOUT UNFORGIVENESS..........................15
UNFORGIVENESS...16
LET'S POINT OUT THE LIE..17
FORGIVE MYSELF...22
HOW TO LOVE ME...24
WHITE ROSE..25
PRETTY GIRL AFFIRMATION ANTHEM.............................28
GUARD MY HEART..31
THE "FATHER" OF ANOTHER BACKGROUND...................35
WHAT IS A FRIEND?..42
LETTER TO WHO YOU ARE AND WHO YOU ARE GOING TO BE...44
SELFLOVE..44

MONEY 45
LIVE IN THE MOMENT 46
EDUCATION 46
FALLING FOR MR. WRONG 48
RELATIONSHIP 53
PRETTY GIRL DAILY DOSE OF INSPIRATION 56
DECLARE & DECREE 138
SPECIAL THANK YOU 140
TAKE THE PRETTY GIRL AFFIRMATION ANTHEM CHALLENGE ... 141
ABOUT THE AUTHOR 142

The Ugly Truth

Confidence stood in the lobby waiting for her best friend, Fearfully doubtful to arrive.

"Are you ready Fd," asked Confidence as she approached Fearfully doubtful.

Fd tugged on her backpack. "Yes."

They double checked their supplies and followed their hiking instructor, Kimberly, across the rocky trail. Words couldn't explain their excitement to finally scratch mountain climbing off their bucket list. All of a sudden Kimberly held up her hand, ordering them to stop. "Sorry, guys look like a detour. We have to climb the mountain in front of us to get to the other side," said Kimberly.

Confidence and the instructor prepared to climb the mountain while Fd scanned her surroundings for an alternate route. Earlier when Fd received the supplies along with specific instructions and techniques to successfully climb the mountain, she was ecstatic. Having Confidence and being accompanied by an experienced hiking instructor was a bonus.

Confidence and Kimberly were halfway up the mountain when they noticed Fd wasn't behind them. They encouraged her to climb, but nothing worked. She didn't know climbing a mountain would be so intimidating. She wondered what happen to her enthusiasm. She figured it climbed the mountain without her and was long gone by now. Both Confidence and Kimberly returned to the bottom of the mountain and joined Fd. Confidence agreed to carry Fd if Kimberly would help, but the instructor refused.

"It would not only be dangerous to do so, but it wouldn't be beneficial for Fd," she added.

They had more mountains to climb and if Fd didn't learn to climb the mountain on her own, they would have to carry her over each one.

Change the way you see you

After hours of standing in the same spot trying to get Fd to climb the mountain, they all agreed it would be best if they went back to the welcome center. A phenomenal motivational speaker will inspire you to climb mountains. Sadly, this means nothing. Your feet will never leave the ground if you don't believe you can do it. You can get pumped up to do anything, but it's still up to you after the cheering stops. What mountains are you facing that's stopping you from changing the way you see you?

Change the way you see you

Watch what you say

Stick and stones may break my bones, but words may never hurt me. It takes a minimum of six to eight weeks for a broken bone to heal, but sometimes it takes a lifetime to heal from hurtful words. Whenever my siblings shouted mean things like you're not my sister, you're stupid, dumb, ugly, baldhead scallywag, I wish you were never born and a list of other things. My response would be, "sticks and stones may break my bones, but your words will never hurt me", or "whatever you say bounces off of me and goes back to you." It sounded like the right thing to say in response to someone being mean, but it was beyond the truth.

When I matured, I discovered the meaning of the saying. I can choose what I allow to hurt me. At that moment I promised myself when I had children of my own, I wouldn't say hurtful things to them. There were words that stuck with me as I got older. These words tormented me. "You will never be anything when you grow up", or "you're slower than molasses in the summer." When I was in the seventh grade, I remember not going to my assigned class. Instead I went to lunch. My peers later told me that when the teacher found out I skipped class, she said I was slower than molasses in the summer. I didn't know what that meant at the time, but I knew it was bad. I later found out it meant I was dumb.

Most times what people say about us hurts because we agree with what they are saying, or we love the person and are hurt that they would say something so hurtful to us. What my teacher said about me was hurtful because most times I didn't feel like I was smart. Here it is twenty years later and I still remember what she said, but I don't remember her name. For years, whenever I tried to do something new, and it seemed hard or difficult, I remembered what she said. I didn't have anyone to tell me I was smart, that I could do anything I put my mind to, I wasn't average, or that I was special. For those very reasons, I poured my heart.

into this book because I don't want you to be like I was.

Even if someone says hurtful things about you, even if no one says you can do it, you will tell yourself that nothing anyone says about you will hurt you. It may sting, but you won't allow it to stop you from being the best YOU possible. Stick and stones may break your bones, but their words will never hurt you.

Who are you?

Do you know who you are? Most people don't know who they are. Before the hike, Kimberly, the hiking instructor, told Confidence and Fd that it would be impossible to climb the mountain they plan to climb. She stated that one has to be really good to climb the mountain. Not many people have done it.

"It must be hard if only a few people did it. You are right: I can't climb the mountain. I'm not strong, and I lack experience," said Fd.

"Get your pen ready to add me to the list of those who did it. I'm sure I can figure it out. If I practice, I know I can do it. I can do anything I put my mind to," said Confidence.

Which describes you when faced with a situation that doesn't seem possible?

Do you act like Confidence or Fd?

This book will help you discover who you are and help you change the way you see you.

When you know who you are, you know what you are not. I can't do that. People who say they can't do something is right, 9 times out of 10 they have never tried, either. If they tried and failed, they didn't keep trying until they could do it.

There are advantages to knowing who you are. Most will say that Confidence was arrogant because of what she said.

Not at all. Confidence was speaking based on what she has done before. She knows she can do anything she puts her mind to. Confidence knows she can't lose. She believes you only lose when you don't try.

Fd probably has been told that she couldn't do something most of her life, and instead of proving whomever even herself wrong, she chose to roll with it. Now when faced with something hard, she automatically says she can't do it. Sadly, she has programmed herself to think she can't do anything hard and she has no desire to try.

Change the way you see you

Do you know who you are? A few years ago, I wouldn't have been able to answer this question.

Why? Because I compared myself to other people. Instead of saying that, "oh they did it so can I", I felt the total opposite: "oh they did it. It must be something special about them."

I learned that we are all special, and if I want to do something, I can do it. It may take me a little more time to get the answer to that math problem, but guess what eventually I'm going to get it if I keep trying and don't give up.

I don't believe there is anything on this earth I can't do. If I want to lose weight, I can. If I want to drive an 18-wheeler truck, I can. I can do all these things with proper training, practice and hard work.

You can do anything. Things always seem impossible until you see someone else do it or you do it yourself.

Today, if someone asked who I am, I'll tell them.

I am a child of God who can do all things through Him. I am chosen, I am special, cherished, a royal priesthood. I am powerful, and everything I touch prospers.

I'm allergic to losing; that's why I strive to win at everything I do. I am more precious than rubies.

I wasn't ALWAYS this STRONG. I had to OVERCOME somethings.

-Starr Coburn

Pretty Girl,

Forgive Quickly & Often.

Don't allow unforgiveness to control you.

Why should I forgive her?

Helen told everyone in school that the wet spot on Jasmine's pants was pee, when in fact, it wasn't pee, it was a juice stain. Now, no one wants to be around her. They even call her names and talk about her behind her back. While Jasmine was eating at lunch, she accidentally spilled juice on her pants. She ran to the bathroom to dry her pants with the hand dryer. She didn't realize the juice would stain her pants. The stain was so big, she couldn't hide it. She had no change of clothes, and the second bell had rung. Jasmine had made it halfway through the day hoping no one would notice her pants, but then she heard it.

"Here." Kelly, Jasmine's friend, took off her jacket and wrapped it around Jasmine, covering up the stain on her pants.
"Thanks. Where were you earlier?"
"My mom dropped me off late." Kelly replied.
"I don't think anyone noticed." Jasmine smiled.
"I'm not so sure about that." She showed Jasmine a picture of her posted on a social media site. Jasmine read it out loud.
"'We aren't in preschool anymore. Why is she still peeing on herself?'"
Jasmine handed the phone back to Kelly. "I'm going to say something bad about her."
"It's not worth it. Why don't you tell the principal so she can get in trouble? That's considered bullying."
Kelly shook her head. "I'm not a snitch."
"Well you may as well forgive her and go on about your day."

CHANGE THE WAY YOU SEE YOU

The bell rang and Jasmine and Kelly went to class.

"Pop quiz!" said the teacher as she placed the papers on the students' desk.

Helen looked over at Jasmine and laughed.

Jasmine was furious. Time had past, and the teacher went around to collect the papers.

"I'll give the papers back to you before class is over. Open your books and read the first chapter and answer questions in the back of the book."

When class was over, Jasmine's teacher, Mrs. Foster, asked her to stay after the class.

"Yes, Mrs. Foster you ask me to stay?"

"Have a seat."

"Am I in trouble?"

"Yes and no."

"Here is your test." She handed Jasmine her test.

"Forty percent?" Jasmine's mouth dropped. My parents are going to kill me."

"This isn't like you. Want to tell me what's going on?"

"No, not really."

"It's obvious something is wrong, and I can't let you retake the test if I don't know what caused you to score so low."

"Helen did."

How did Helen cause you to do poorly on your test?"

"I couldn't concentrate."

"Was she making noises?"

"No, earlier today I found out that Helen spread a rumor about me. I couldn't stop thinking about what she did."

"You have to forgive her and don't think about it anymore."

"But it's hard. Everyone is talking about me and it's

because of her."

"Jasmine, Helen may have been the first to spread a rumor about you, but she won't be the last. People can be cruel. As my grandmother would say, 'You have to have tough skin'."

"I don't want tough skin."

"Not physically but mentally. Meaning, no matter what people say you will not let it affect how you live your life. When Helen said those things, it hurt and it controlled your life from the time you heard about it up until now."

"How?"

"You couldn't focus on your test because you were thinking about what she said. You probably thought of many ways to get back at her."

Jasmine laughed. "How did you know?"

"That's a natural reaction. To get back at someone for doing something to you."

"You said that I should forgive her. Will that stop me from thinking about what she did?"

Mrs. Foster shook her head. "You control what you think about. You can think about what she did and get upset all over again, or you can think about something that makes you happy and have a good day."

"Okay, thanks Mrs. Foster!"

"No problem. You can retake the test Friday."

Jasmine saw Helen go to the bathroom and followed her. When Helen came out of the stall, Jasmine was standing at the sink waiting on her.

Helen walked to the sink and washed her hands.

"Helen, I know what you said about me, and I don't like it," Jasmine started.

"I wanted to fight you because you made me look bad

and everyone was talking about me, but I forgive you."

Helen was quiet and Jasmine continued talking. "I'll appreciate it if you don't say mean things about me. I could have told the principal what you did, and I'm sure you would have gotten suspended and possibly kicked off the cheerleading team for bullying, but I didn't."

Helen was still silent. "You shouldn't do things to others that you don't want done to you." said Jasmine.

Helen turned off the water and dried her hands. "Whatever, if I say you peed on yourself you did. Deal with it." Helen smiled and walked past Jasmine and out of the bathroom.

Jasmine felt herself getting upset. She started thinking about what happened earlier. She thought about her talk with Mrs. Foster and stopped her thoughts of Helen.

She shook her head. "Some people are just mean. I wonder what Mom is cooking for dinner."

Jasmine was able to enjoy the rest of her day and do great in her classes.

BROKEN

Have you ever talked to someone who was rude or mean? It bothered you so much that you had to ask, "who hurt you?"

I've learned that if you listen long enough, people will tell you exactly where they're hurting.

Take a child, for example, who has been taught it's not ok to cry or express their feelings because it's a sign of weakness. Let's say this child falls. When they get back up, they may not say anything about the fall because they have an image to uphold. However, if you watch them, you will see them limping or rubbing the area they hurt when they fell.

We are no different. We may look put together on the outside, but some of us are hurt and broken on the inside.

Sometimes we try to appear as we have it all together, not knowing that our brokenness is seeping through, whether it is how we treat others or how we treat ourselves.

Quote: When you are looking through the broken glass it's hard to see how beautiful you are.

-When you look through a broken glass, you see a bunch of imperfect pieces that can't be put back together.

-The pieces distract you from seeing who you are.

-Broken glass is meant to be thrown away. You can hurt yourself if you don't.

CHANGE THE WAY YOU SEE YOU

- When you have been broken, whether someone hurt you mentally or physically, it's hard to get over the past hurt and pain. Therefore, we label ourselves as broken.

- We have broken pieces that are preventing us from seeing ourselves how God sees us.

-The broken pieces we have are cutting others we meet because we are hurting.

We know that glass, once it is broken, can't be put it back together. You can't fix glass after it has been broken. You must throw it away. But here's the thing: you aren't glass. No matter how broken you may feel or see yourself, you can be made whole; however, you must see past your brokenness and start the process of healing.

Pretty Girl,
Watch out for broken pieces

When we are hurt by someone, IT'S hard to navigate through the broken glass (heart). Sometimes we find ourselves getting cut all over again. The only way we can heal is to step over the glass and enter into a place where we can't be hurt again.

Some truth about unforgiveness

I know it may seem impossible to forgive someone who hurt you. It makes sense to dislike them or even hate them for what they did to you.

Truth is THAT some people don't know that they hurt you, OR some may know and don't care that they hurt you. Here's the thing: the person who has been hurt tends to suffer the most, not always from what happened to them, but because they didn't forgive the person who hurt them. You're probably thinking why Should I forgive? they are the ones who hurt me.

Change the way you see you

Unforgiveness

Forgiveness doesn't just happen. Like anything else we do, it takes practice. The more you forgive, the better you get at doing it.

Most people are broken because they haven't forgiven the person who caused them to feel broken.

Most haven't forgiven that person because they don't know how, or they don't want to.

They don't want to because they don't feel that a person deserves to be forgiven.

I've learned that unforgiveness doesn't hurt the person who did it. It hurts the person clinging to unforgiveness. It destroys us mentally, physically, and spiritually.

Think about it: when that person comes around-- you know, that person that you have been holding a grudge against since high school or even a few seconds ago? What's the first thing you do? You think about what they did, and the way you felt when they did it surface. Now you're mad, sad, and you can't function.

You're not bothered for a minute. Your whole day is ruined because you took yourself back to the crime scene. You know when they wronged you. They knew what they did, and You told yourself it would be a cold day in you know what before you forgive them.

We must forgive from the heart.

Let's Point Out the Lie

When you forgive someone, you don't automatically forget about it.

As long as we think about it, the pain will never go away. The moment you stop thinking about something and focus on something else, you forget whatever it was they did.

Why do you think about it? You think about it because there is a wound that won't heal because you keep pulling back the scab. When we pull back the scab, we have to let it heal again. There are dangers to pulling back the scab. It can get infected. Once it gets infected, you must undergo treatment to remove the infection.

I had a c-section with my first child. My doctor sent me home with strict instructions to follow. I didn't follow them, and I ended up back in the hospital. While in the hospital, the doctors said they had to open my wound back up because it may have gotten infected, and this time, I had to heal from the inside out.

Some of our unforgiveness runs deep from childhood to adulthood. So deep that it's now rooted. So, in order to get rid of it, you must undergo surgery so you can heal from the inside out.

Change the way you see you

Well how do I forgive?

Repent for not forgiving

Ask God.

-to create in you a clean heart and a right spirit.

- to reveal the root of it.

-to walk with you as you forgive because it's not always easy.

You need to identify what the person did down to every detail. Sometimes you will find you can't remember what they did or that the thing they did wasn't even that bad.

Example: They hurt me. When I needed them the most, they weren't there for me. I was there for them. I'm always the one people call on, but when I need help nobody helps me.

No one's there for Starr when she needs them.

What you should do physically:

-Dig deep, write down everything this person did to you. You need to know what they did so you know what you are forgiving them for. This may be painful, but it's necessary.

-Go to that person and tell them how you feel about what happened in private.

C̲h̲a̲n̲g̲e̲ ̲t̲h̲e̲ ̲w̲a̲y̲ ̲y̲o̲u̲ ̲s̲e̲e̲ ̲y̲o̲u̲

-Keep in mind that everybody will not be pleased with you comforting them. Think about the right words to say.

-Let them know you forgive them.

You don't have to be friends or associate after that.

-Separate the clean from the unclean. If this person is causing harm to you than they would be consider unclean. Don't let them keep doing it. Fool me once shame on you fool you twice shame on me.

My hope is that we have so much wisdom and decrement that people don't have a chance of hurting us.

Pray for them. Be nice.

Things will come about and trigger your thoughts on what happen, what they did. Stop your thoughts before it gets to that. Think about something else. No, I forgave them. I'm not thinking on that and don't think on it find something else to think about. I wonder what I'm going to eat for lunch anything but them.

Practice, Practice, Practice. You are going to encounter people who do wrong by you and it's going to require forgiveness.

Some people miss out on opportunities because they won't forgive. Don't let that be you. You can forgive, but you must want to. Forgiving is hard to do says most people. I say, It's not hard. We have been taught that forgiving is hard. But anything is hard if you don't want to do it.

When I dealt with unforgiveness.

This person did something to me and I hated them for it

It had gotten so bad that I hated to hear their voice. I would cringe to the point I could punch a wall or them.

One day I was talking to this person and they said, "why can't we just talk without you lashing out on me? You always quoting scriptures, you're so holy and you can't even hold a conversation with me without getting mad or hanging up."

I thought, seriously? They did not try to pull my saint card. I wanted to believe they were trying to make me feel bad. Sadly, they were right. I quoted scriptures, and I was ready to lay hands on them, but not to pray.

So, I had to do some soul searching. I knew I wanted to be like my Father in heaven, so I got into my Word to find out how He was. He loved; He forgave. And I knew I had to do the same.

Now, forgiving can be difficult when you have people in your ear telling you that if they were you, they wouldn't forgive, or they would tell you that, that person doesn't deserve to be forgiven. You have a right to be mad. While you have all right, the Word says be anger but sin not. I can be mad at what they did, but it becomes a sin when I don't forgive them for what they did.

So, I forgave. It took time. And honestly, when I think about that person, I can't recall why I didn't like them. Oh yes, I can; I just chose to forget about it.

How do you know when you have forgiven someone?

When you see that person and they no longer remind you of the scars they gave you. You know how when you get older, you have scars, but you can't remember how you got them? That's the same feeling you get when you have forgiven someone.

Please forgive. If not for them, most definitely for you. Remember, when you are broken you cut others.

Pretty Girl,
Forgive yourself.

Sometimes it's easier to forgive others for doing something wrong, but we don't forgive ourselves for doing wrong. We punish ourselves by mentally revisiting the thoughts of what happen. Don't be held back because you refuse to forgive yourself.

CHANGE THE WAY YOU SEE YOU

Forgive myself

- Admit you made a mistake.
- Accept what you did, even if it was horrible.
- Apologize to yourself for acting in such away
- Promise yourself that you will never do it again.
- Live as if it never happened. Your past is behind you.
- Don't think about it when thoughts of what happen come up.
- Focus on being a better version of you.

Pretty Girl, I'm sorry for my actions. I should not have acted like that. I'm better than that. I could have done things differently. I feel horrible for doing that. I won't put myself in that type of situation again. It was embarrassing and I feel ashamed. From this day forward, I will not do it again or anything that will make me feel like I'm feeling now. I forgive myself; I'm leaving the past behind me. I won't allow unforgiveness to hold me captive.

Change the way you see you

Pretty Girl,
LOVE YOURSELF

When you love yourself, you teach others how to love you. No one can love you better than you love yourself.

CHANGE THE WAY YOU SEE YOU

How to love me

Take Care of myself.
Eat Healthy.
Exercise.
Style my hair the way I like.
Wear clothes that make me feel great.
Do things that make me happy.
Be patient with myself when I don't get something immediately.
Don't give up on myself.
Be kind to myself.
Never do anything to hurt myself.
When I make a mistake, I don't keep making myself feel bad for doing it.
I protect myself from being hurt by others mentally, physically, and emotionally.
I reward myself for doing good and achieving goals.
I don't dishonor myself by calling myself bad names.
I trust myself to love me unconditional because no one can love me like I love me.

CHANGE THE WAY YOU SEE YOU

WHITE ROSE

It was the first day of summer camp. The kids gathered around the campfire for the welcome ceremony. The camp leader, Zac, instructed the kids to take turns introducing themselves and tell one thing that they loved about themselves. Zac pulled a white rose from a basket. All the kids gasped and said how pretty it was. Some had never seen a white rose before.

Zac held up the rose and began to speak. "By a show of hands, how many have seen a white rose before?"

A couple of campers raised their hand.

"How many have seen a red rose?" asked Zac.

Everyone raised their hand.

"Roses are very expensive. They come in many shades and smell lovely. The red rose symbolizes love. That's why so many red roses are sold during Valentine's Day. Who can tell me what the white rose symbolizes?"

Zac called on a student. "Clean. Anything white means its clean. At least that's what my mom says."

Zac nodded. "That's right. This white rose symbolizes clean, which is another word for purified, innocence, honor, reverence, a new beginning, and everlasting love. I'm sending the rose around. Look at it and pass it to the next person. What do you like about the rose?"

The campers laughed and played while they passed the rose around. Some of them were gentle, while a lot of the boys were rough. They broke a couple of pieces of the stem and removed some of the petals when Zac wasn't looking.

The last person to touch the rose gave it to Zac, and he put the rose back in the bag. He pulled out another rose, but this time, the rose had glass over it. He passed the rose around. Most careful not to break the glass shielding the rose, while some tried removing the glass, but they couldn't because it was sealed tight. The last person handed the rose to Zac.

Zac took the other rose out of the bag. He held both roses in his hand.

"Which rose has a better chance of surviving? The rose in the glass or the rose without the glass?"

"With the glass," they shouted.

"You guys are correct. The rose in the glass has been shielded from all dangers that may come its way; whereas, the rose without the glass will die because it has been exposed to a hostile environment. The rose probably died the moment John broke the stem," said Zac.

John's eyes and mouth popped open.

"Imagine your life as this rose." Zac held up the rose without a glass. The stem was the size of a fingernail. It had way fewer petals than before. It was no longer white but had a dingy look to it.

Change the Way You See You

"As you go through life unprotected, people are going to treat you like this rose. Before you know it, you will be mentally and physically broken, and you will not be happy with yourself. When you are not happy with yourself, it leads to self-hate, depression, stress, suicidal thoughts or actions. You will hate people and have a hard time trusting others, out of fear they will hurt you."

He crumbled the rose and sprinkled it over the ground. He held the rose in the glass with two hands. "Why do you think this rose looks the same every time someone touched it?"

John raised his hand. "We couldn't touch it because it was underneath the glass."

"Correct." Said Zac. "Because the rose was protected by the glass, nothing could get in to harm the rose-- destroy its beauty."

Zac continued. "That's how you must be with yourself. You must protect the precious rose that you are. Don't allow anyone to mishandle you. People will come and try to get you to remove the glass, but don't do it. They can destroy everything you are and plan to be."

Pretty Girl,
Know your worth!

I have never known of anyone going into a restaurant and negotiating the price of food. The price that is listed is the price you pay. The restaurant owner knows the value of their food and the quality of their service. They know how much time and effort goes into making the dish. You either pay or go somewhere else. If someone really wants the food, they will pay the price, regardless of the cost. Don't allow people to downplay you. Know your worth.

Change the way you see you

Pretty girl affrimation anthem

I am not loud, stupid, poor.

I am far from ugly, crazy, irritating.

I am more than the bad names they blurt out about me.

I am not alone. I'm surrounded by people who love me.

I LOVE, RESPECT, CHERISH, and ACCEPT myself exactly as I am.

I am beautiful and wonderfully made.

I am intelligent, confident, and important.

I am a kind, creative, leader.

I am courageous.

I am phenomenal--no need to compare myself to others.

I can do anything I put my mind to.

EVERYTHING I touch PROSPERS!

I woke up a winner. I don't quit.

I am and will always be AMAZING.

You **HOLD** the KEY to the door that **LEADS** to your **HEART**.

— STARR COBURN

Pretty Girl,
GUARD YOUR HEART.

Not everyone deserves a spare key to unlock it.

CHANGE THE WAY YOU SEE YOU

Guard My Heart

When Jenna became a teenager, she knew her parents would see her as responsible and finally give her the key to the house. Everyone had a key-- her big brother, her younger sister, even her aunt who stayed a thousand miles away had a key. Jenna told her mother that she didn't want just any oh regular key. No, she had high expectations. She wanted her key to be her favorite color, pink and have lots of flowers. Jenna was devastated when her mother told her that she couldn't get the key she wanted; in fact, she wasn't getting a key at all. She didn't understand why her mother wouldn't give her a key to the house. She felt like an outsider; she was the only one without a key.

She figured if their dog, Max, could open the door, he would also have a key. After walking around the house pouting for about a week, Jenna's mother sat down with her.

"Jenna I would love to give you a key, but I don't think you are ready."

"Mom, it's just a key."

"Yes, it may just seem like a key, but that key is used to unlock the door to our home, our safe place."

"I know, Mom, but I promise I will not lose the key."

"I'm not worried about you losing the key. I'm concerned with what you do once you get in the house."

Jenna looked puzzled.

"Jenna, when you come in the house, you never lock the door behind you. This is dangerous because anybody can come into our house and take what they want. They won't take little things like a spoon or fork. They will take the valuable stuff. The stuff that cost the most. When they take these things, it will leave us heart broken."

"We can buy new stuff."

"You're right, but we won't feel safe in our home anymore."

"Mom, I promise I won't let that happen. For now on, I will double check to make sure the door is locked because I don't want any one coming in to take our stuff.

"Ok, Jenna. I'll take your word for it." Her mom reached into her pocket and gave Jenna a pink key covered in flowers.

Jenna didn't see the importance of the key aside from the key is the only way to get in the house. She didn't understand the value of what the key protected. Someone has to first get permission from you to enter your heart.

Change the way you see you

How to Guard My Heart

We open our heart to people who make us feel great. If someone says something nice to make us feel good, help us when we are in trouble, or do nice things for us just because. We tend to open the door to our heart more quickly.

It's hard to open the door to someone who is mean to us.

If you find that you have given your heart to someone mean, it's because at some point, they were nice enough to you for you to let them into your heart.

Sadly, trying to retrieve the spare key you gave them becomes almost impossible.

Before you start making spare keys to your heart and giving them away, you need to build a firewall. A firewall will help to keep everyone out that could infect you with a virus (Break your heart).

Everyone who calls you pretty, says something nice, or does something nice for you does not deserve a key to your heart, especially if you've just met them.

Watch how this person treats other people. Are they nice to other people? Do they say nice things about other people? If they are mean to other people, they are capable of being mean to you.

Are they always nice to you, or do they want something from you for being nice to you?

Change the way you see you

The "Father" of Another Background

YOU were my FATHER at once I knew,
But little do you know the PAIN you put me through.
I've GROWN up and realized that your life is nothing but One THOUSAND lies.
I'm 13 now, we should be tied, instead I have only CRIED.
I know you have your wife and you LOVE her I'm sure, but don't forget we share the same BLOOD line too.
But obviously that DOESN'T mean ANYTHING to you. Out the corner of my eye he left one day without saying GOODBYE.
YOU say my MOM is standing in the way, and all she wants is for you to pay.
Maybe that's true, but what can I do?
I'm your daughter too.
You're supposed to be my father. Does that MEAN anything to you?
You will NEVER see and a father you will never be. If you could see the tears running down my face. Still years have PASSED, you cannot replace.
For nine years I sat and stared wondering about the DAD who never cared. What if I was the girl who lost EVERYTHING, the one who was left with nothing.
How would you FEEL? You said we were a MISTAKE, you made us feel like we weren't a big deal.
In TIME this all will HEAL.
You claim I'm your daughter, but this goes to my "FATHER"
I'm the DAUGHTER you have ABANDONED.
From now on, I will just call you BRANDON.

POEM BY
- DIAMOND TAYLOR

Change the way you see you

Pretty Girl,

WIPE your eyes, there is no need to CRY.
I promise everything will be alright.
I know it HURTS and right now you're probably calling him a JERK.
He's too BLIND to see your WORTH.
You are not alone you are cherished and loved by others. You are not a MISTAKE the biggest MISTAKE was him not being in your life.
You are enough. You aren't worthless, yet PRICELESS. It's not your FAULT he's not around. It's WRONG that you have to go through this, and the hardest thing to tell you is to be STRONG. You can't change what was, but you can change what will be. You will be AMAZING. You will do GREAT things. You will not be held captive by the thoughts of the unknown, in spite of his absence.
Look at you, you're doing WONDERFUL. You are accomplishing things you never thought you could. REPLACE the void in your life with more love for yourself. At times his absence will bring great sorrow, but PRETTY GIRL, don't let it rob you of your tomorrow.

Pretty Girl,

That's not your friend.

Anyone can say they are your friend, but it's more to friendship than just saying it. Everyone who says they are your friend may not be. Be careful who you tell your secrets to.

Pretty Girl,

Everyone will not like you!

There may be individuals that dislike you. That's ok. It has nothing to do with you, but them. There is something they don't admire about themselves, and you remind them of who they are not or they desire to be. You like you, and that's all that matters.

Pretty Girl,

Surround yourself with like- minded people.

Your associates should be ambitious, goal oriented, nice, loving, caring, just like you. If you hang around people who don't have the same or similar qualities as you, they can stop you from being the best you can be. The people we hang around can help us be great, or they can be the reason we are not great.

Pretty Girl,

Do an assessment on every person who you call friend. Are they helping you be great or preventing you from being great?

CHANGE THE WAY YOU SEE YOU

Pretty Girl,

Life is like a sport. The field is yours. You choose who plays on it, so choose your team carefully. Not everyone wants to see you win.

Change the way you see you

What is a friend?

A friend is someone with whom you share a bond.
A friend will allow you to express your feelings without judging you.
A friend doesn't call you bad names like stupid, ugly, dirty, fat, lazy, etc.
A friend laughs with you, not at you, unless you said something hilarious.
A friend will support you.
A friend helps you solve problems.
A friend will be there for you when you need them.
A friend cheers you up when you are feeling sad.
A friend encourages you and pushes you to be the best.
A friend will never be jealous of you.
A friend will never let anyone talk bad about you.
A friend will never make fun of you.
A friend doesn't say bad things about you, to you, or to others.
A friend keeps your secrets.
A friend helps you even when you don't want them to help you.
A friend is like a sister/brother.
A friend doesn't lie to you.
A friend protects you.
A friend tells you the truth, even if it may hurt because they want what's best for you.
A friend will never humiliate you in front of others.
You may have disagreement, but a friend will never say or do anything to hurt you when they get mad at you.

Change the way you see you

A friend will not allow you to embarrass yourself.
A friend loves you no matter what.

To attract friends one must first show themselves friendly.

CHANGE THE WAY YOU SEE YOU

LETTER TO WHO YOU ARE AND WHO YOU ARE GOING TO BE

Life—well, life can be tough. It will knock you down, but you must get back up. Here are some things I, along with other women, have learned along the way, in hopes you won't make the same mistakes.

Selflove
Dear Pretty Girl,

You only live once and get one body. Take care of yourself, eat healthy, and exercise. Be more respectful and responsible with your body. Eating junk food and fast food doesn't seem to have a visible effect on you now, but it will as you get older. Your metabolism slows down, you will add on pounds, and possibly develop diabetes, high blood pressure, or other harmful diseases that come with eating unhealthily and not exercising. Protect your skin from the sun. Wear good bras. Take care of your hair. You are not fat or too skinny. Don't be so negative on yourself.

Don't be afraid to stand up for yourself. If someone is harming or is making you feel uncomfortable-- if you don't feel you can stop them, tell your mom what's happening to you or tell someone you trust, so they can help you.

Don't put drugs in your body. Drugs don't love you. They won't fix your problems; they will add to them. You can think better without alcohol. There will always be someone that looks better, dress better, etc. none of that matters because you will not compare yourself to others. Find out who you are in Christ.

Don't be afraid. Don't listen to the negative thoughts inside your head telling you to be quiet. Go, make your dreams come true. Once you find out who you are, accept it and love it. Self-care and self-love are essential. Live your truth. Don't be afraid to be yourself and to be true to yourself. Try your best. You are enough and worth far more than you may think. Be happy. Be patient. Don't be envious. Mistakes don't make you a failure. It's ok to fail; just learn from it. Learn to say no.

Don't get wrapped up with what people think or say about you. You can move mountains. Think long term before you decide. Read daily affirmations. Learn to love yourself sooner than later. Tell yourself how much you love yourself and why you love you. Be comfortable with yourself. Take time to pamper yourself by polishing your nails, taking a long soothing bubble bath, listening to soft music to clear your mind and reflect on who you are and the things you desire to accomplish. Have a girl's day with friends or family who make you uplift your spirit. Buy yourself something it doesn't matter if it's big or small if you love it.

Don't depend on others to make you happy; do it yourself. When life gets overwhelming and you feel stressed or depressed, talk to someone who can help you cope with the way you are feeling. Know that you will be stronger, smarter and more amazing than everyone said you would ever be.

Money
Dear Pretty Girl,

When you are able, and it doesn't affect your education, get a job. Make your own money. Your credit is gold. Pay your bills on time, and owe no one. Manage your money; don't spend everything you get. Always pay yourself when you get paid and put aside savings. Don't get a lot of student loans and credit cards. Get one credit card to build your credit. If you can't afford to pay cash, you can't afford it. Save until you can afford to get what you want. Don't buy things to impress people. Invest your money, buy stock, properties, or franchises when you are young. Save for your future. Make money. Save money. Live in financial peace now so you won't have to struggle when you get older. Don't be in a rush to be on your own. Stay with your parents as long as you need in order to save.

Live in the moment
Dear Pretty Girl,

Just wait! You have plenty of time, so stop rushing everything. Wait to have kids; enjoy your life while it's just you. Make time for family and friends you love. Tell them that you love them. Do things a little bit at a time. Do more while you are young. Trust the process. Don't rush your progress. Trials and situations will come, but God will always be there to carry you through it. Have fun. Do everything, and try new things at least once. Even if you are scared, do it anyway. Don't miss out on opportunities because you are shy. Travel; don't get stuck in the state you were born in. There's a beautiful world to explore.

Education
Dear Pretty Girl,

Don't drop out of school. Good grades matter. Stay in your

books. It seems right and fun to follow friends, but your education comes first. Look into all your options for career choices. Pick up your violin and never stop practicing. Study hard. Invest in yourself. Gain more knowledge, and never stop learning. Stay focused. Keep going. Finish what you started so you don't have to finish later. If you want to go to college, go. If you don't feel college is for you, enroll in a trade school or start your own business. Do something that will allow you to have a prosperous future.

Always remember that no one owes you anything. If you want something, you must work hard to get it. You are responsible for creating the life you desire.

Change the way you see you

Falling for Mr. Wrong

Samantha and Nekita sat at the round table in the cafeteria at school. Nekita moved closer to Samantha. "Did you see how Jonathan looked at you?"

"No," Samantha replied.

"Sis, he couldn't take his eyes off of you." Samantha shrugged and went back to reading her history book.

"I think you should talk to him. I mean, if he asks you to be his girlfriend, you should say yes."

"Why? I don't have time for a boyfriend. My dad say boys are nothing but trouble, and I should stay away from them. My education is more important."

Samantha shrugged. "Yeah, my mom said the same thing and so did my brother, but that didn't stop me from dating Shawn."

Samantha glanced at Nekita and continuing to read.

"You probably should have listened to them. Shawn is a jerk, and he doesn't care about you."

"How can you say that? Shawn loves me. He tells me all of the time." Nekita smiled.

The bell rang. Nekita jumped up from her seat. "My stomach hurts," she moaned before vomiting on the floor.

Samantha stood up dodging the vomit. She grabbed paper towels from the table and gave them to Nekita. "Are you ok?" a teacher asked.

Nekita wiped her mouth and stood up. "Yes, ma'am."

"Go to the nurse so she can check your temperature," said the teacher.

Change the Way You See You

"Can I go with her?" Samantha asked.

The teacher nodded. Samantha and Nekita went to the bathroom to wash their hands.

"I wonder what made you throw up. You didn't eat anything during lunch."

"I ate some hot chips during last period," Nekita explained, "but that's not what made me throw up."

They left the bathroom.

"Samantha," Nekita started. "Why did you say you didn't like Shawn?"

Samantha looked at her. "I didn't say I didn't like him. I said he was a jerk. Why does it matter what I think? You don't listen to anyone when it comes to him."

Nekita looked down as they walked down the hall.

"Nekita," Samantha said, "you are my best friend, and I wouldn't tell you anything wrong. You deserve better than Shawn. I know he is cute, and all the girls want to be with him, but he calls you out of your name. You get upset if your brother calls you stupid or curse you, but when Shawn does it, you laugh."

"He's just playing. He doesn't mean it."

"Well, I don't like it. Love doesn't call names or make fun of you. Not to mention, he hit you."

Nekita shook her head. "That was an accident."

"How can you accidentally hit someone in the face and cause them to bruise? If it was an accident, why did you tell your brother we were playing, and I accidentally hit you?"

"I didn't want him to try to fight Shawn."

"My dad said when a boy hits you, that means

he doesn't love you. Only cowards hit girls."

"Whenever he hits me, I hit him back. We fight each other."

Samantha stopped. "I thought you said he only hit you once and it was an accident."

Nekita stared at Samantha.

"I can't tell you what to do or who to date, but I'm begging you to stop dating him. We only hang out at school because he doesn't let you go anywhere. He talks to other girls. I know you know, and I don't know why you allow this. You are failing your first period class because you are coming to school late to be with him."

"I know, "Nekita sighed. "I'm going to do better."

"Speaking of school-- He doesn't even go. You know that, right?"

"He said he's going to get his GED."

"I don't even know who you are anymore. The Nekita I know wouldn't let a boy come between her and her education. I miss hearing you talk about what you are going to do once you get your Ph.D. and open your own practice. You said I would be your accountant because I have great math skills."

"We still can." Nekita held her stomach.

"We should go to the nurse," Samantha touched Nekita's back.

Nekita shook her head. "I just need to sit down."

They walked over to the stairway and sat down.

"Shawn has been doing better. I'm working with him to change," Nekita said.

"Change? Nekita, you can't change him. He has to want to change. It's not him that's changing; it's you, and I don't like it."

CHANGE THE WAY YOU SEE YOU

Nekita received a text. She read it as Samantha looked on.

"No." Samantha snatched Nekita's phone.

"Give it back!" Nekita pleaded.

"No, you are not leaving school to go be with him." She stood up and replied to the text and dropped the phone in her pocket.

"What did you text him?"

"I told him that you will not be able to make it, that you have a test. You will call him later."

"He's going to be mad."

Samantha shrugged. "Oh well. Shawn does not love you. How can you not see that? He wants you to leave school. That means you will miss class and get another absence. I've been holding my tongue because I don't want to hurt your feelings. But if I'm your friend and I love you, I have to tell you what's right, no matter if it will hurt your feelings. I'm telling you the truth in love."

Nekita shook her head, tears in her eyes, but Samantha went on.

"From the moment you introduced me to Shawn I knew he wasn't right for you, but I didn't want to upset you. I didn't want you to think I was hating on you. I covered for you. I told your mom you were at my house when you were with him. I did your work and turned it in with mine when you didn't come to class because I didn't want you to fail. I'm not doing it anymore. Shawn does not love you. When you love someone, you don't hurt them with words or your hands. When you love someone and you are in a relationship, you don't have other girlfriends or boyfriends. When you love someone, you push them to be a better person, to do good, not bad."

Change the way you see you

Nekita wiped the tears away from her face.

Samantha hugged Nekita. "I'm not telling you this to make you feel bad, but because I want to see you do better."

"What are you doing in the hall, Miss Samantha?" asked the assistant principal.

"She was taking me to the nurse, said Nekita. "I threw up earlier. My stomach started hurting again, so we sat down until it stopped."

"Okay, don't be too long. You are missing valuable information. Well, then again, you both are honor students, so I'm sure you wouldn't have a problem catching up. I hope you feel better, Nekita." The assistant principal walked away.
Nekita stood up. "Let's get going."
They started down the hall.
Samantha hugged Nekita again. "I don't want you to be stuck with him for the rest of your life."

"But I am." Nekita held her stomach and sobbed.

Relationship
Dear Pretty Girl,

When you get older and you know and love who you are, and you don't compromise, and you feel like you are ready for a relationship, first talk to your parents or guardian about it. Know why you want to let this person into your life, and it shouldn't be because he is so cute, he can dress, or he is popular. He can be all of those things and be a jerk.

Too many times, we allow our emotions to override what is right. We ignore the red flags. It's natural for you to like a boy. However, it's important that the boy you like will not destroy your life. Everyone doesn't deserve your time. Never ever let a boy put his hands on you to hurt you. Make sure he doesn't talk bad to you or about you. That's not love; that's hate. Save yourself because the wrong one will make you lose yourself. Learn what love is, practice it, become familiar with it. If he doesn't show love, run and don't look back.

You cannot change people. Don't spend time trying to change someone because you will change in the long run, and it may not be for the better. In every situation, you must use wisdom. If it's not right, walk away because he's not worth it, and you deserve better.

Stay away from toxic people. Don't base your self-worth on whether boys think you are pretty. Know that you are pretty.

Change the way you see you

You can't make everyone happy. Pay attention to your intuition, that gut feeling you have that something is not right. It's probably not, and you need to figure out what it is before it's too late.

Get your education, and get your own money. Don't rush love. Boys will always be around. Make sure he doesn't have a girlfriend. Don't become comfortable with being second to anyone. He should be with you and only you. You and your friends may share a lot of things but a male? Never.

Be sure that he is kind. Make sure he is not controlling, telling you what you can and can't do, keeping you away from friends and family. Make sure he isn't jealous because a jealous person can be dangerous. If he loves you, he will make time to spend with you, put you before his friends, and introduce you to his mother. You can learn a bit about him by watching how he treats his mother. He will never pressure or manipulate you into doing anything you don't want to do. Remember, love is not just a word, it's an action. Let him meet your friends. Ask your friends, parents, or someone you trust what they think about him. Sometimes we get so blinded by love, we can't see how people really are. The good ones will push you to be better; they won't distract you from being a better you.

Think with your brain and not your emotions. Have high standards because not everyone deserves your love. Watch who you decide to spend your life with and build a family with. Listen to your mother and your father when it comes to boys. They have experienced a lot, and

CHANGE THE WAY YOU SEE YOU

they can tell if can tell if the person is right for you or not. Your heart doesn't always guide you wisely. Everyone is not with you because they like you. Some will use you to get what they want. Don't let a boy stop you from doing anything that will better you. You're worth more than boys say you are. You may not be in love him, but in love with the way he makes you feel. It's okay to be single and experience life.

Pretty Girl Daily Dose of Inspiration

Read a page everyday
or read all at once.

Day 1

Your desire to achieve your goal has to be stronger than your anxieties convincing you that you will never succeed.

-Starr Coburn

Day 2

Pretty Girl,

Be Kind to Everyone!

When you are kind, you make others feel good.

Day 3

Pretty Girl,

Be Courageous!

When you are confronted with something hard, remember that you are brave. You can accomplish whatever you are seeking to do.

Day 4

Pretty Girl,

Take your time!

Do the best you can. It's ok if it takes you longer than expected to complete. It's most important that you finish. We often get in a hurry to do things because we are competing with others to get the task done. Don't focus on how everyone else is doing; concentrate on you. The more time you spend focusing on someone else, the less time you have to do your best. Just imagine you are the only one that has to complete this project so that you are not distracted by what others are doing.

Day 5

Planted within you is greatness standing by for you to utilize.

-Starr Coburn

Day 6

Pretty Girl,

You Can!

If you think you can't do something, then you are absolutely correct. The main reason we don't do things is that we tell ourselves we can't do it without trying. Instead of saying you can't, say I can and I will and put it into action.

Day 7

Not everyone NEEDS to know the cause of the SCARES in your LIFE. Some people may use what they know about you to wound you.
- STARR COBURN

Day 8

Pretty Girl,

Forget about it!

Forget about your past failures. You can't change what happen, but you can have a better future if you work toward doing better now.

Day 9

Pretty Girl,

Eliminate All Distractions

Don't allow people to distract you from being the best you can be. When people don't want you to succeed, they will do things to distract you so you can't be great. Sometimes the things we love to do, like social media and other things, can distract us from completing important things.

Day 10

Pretty Girl,

Don't Worry

Stop worrying about how far you have to go and appreciate how far you have come. You will get there! Keep moving forward. You got this. I believe in you.

Day 11

Pretty Girl,

Don't Give UP!

It's easy to give up. Keep in mind that you will never win if you give up. Winners never quit, and quitters never win. Think of a time you didn't give up. Do you remember how it made you feel? You can do it again, and again, and again-- if you don't give up.

Day 12

Pretty Girl,

Don't be Ashamed

Of who you are, where you're from or what you did.

Day 13

Pretty Girl,

You can't undo your mistake.

If only we were born with a ginormous eraser to erase all of our mistakes. I'll be happy to say that I've searched everywhere, and I couldn't find it. But I have discovered that although we can't erase our mistakes, we are able to learn from them.

Day 14

It's not HARD to succeed at something new; however, it does take HARDWORK and DEDICATION.
- **STARR COBURN**

Day 15

Pretty Girl,

Life Happens

You will fail
You will succeed
You will think you are not good enough,
You will think you are unstoppable.
You will laugh until your tummy hurts
or until you are gasping for air.
You will ugly cry
You will lose friends and family you love.
You will experience a lot of things. Those are a part of life. You have to remind yourself who you are so that you don't lose yourself in the process.

Day 16

Pretty Girl,

Challenge yourself.

Don't settle for average or safe. Work hard so you can be the best you can be in whatever you do.

Day 17

Pretty Girl,

Stay Prepared.

Your preparation determines your performance. If you don't prepare, you won't perform well.

Day 18

Pretty Girl,

Don't let their opinions stop you.
We miss out on doing things we love because someone else said they didn't like it. Do what makes you happy. If you don't, it will make you unhappy whenever you think about missing the chance of doing that thing.

Day 19

Sometimes the BIGGEST mistake we make is trying to get people to SEE what we SEE.
- STARR COBURN

Day 20

Pretty Girl,

Speak:

-loud and clear.

-your mind as long as it doesn't degrade anyone.

-so that you are heard your opinion matters.

-so they can hear you in the back.

Day 21

Pretty Girl,

Take my word: you will get there. It will happen. I know it seems hard right now, but keep in mind that anything worth having takes hard work and dedication.
You can do it.
Wipe those tears and believe in yourself.

Day 22

Pretty Girl,

It's ok to cry.

Sometimes things happen in our life, and it's going to make us cry.

That's normal.

It doesn't mean you are a cry baby. It doesn't mean you are weak. Cry if you need to. Cry because it's hard. Cry because it's painful. Cry because you don't want to lose. Cry because you lose and you refuse to lose again.

Day 23

The tears may not stop right away, but fight through the tears to get to where you're trying to go or what you are trying to accomplish.

- STARR COBURN

Day 24

Don't drown in your tears; instead, build a boat and use those tears as waves to get you to where you are going.
- STARR COBURN

Day 25

Pretty Girl,

Say no.

It's ok to say no if you don't want to do something that's going to hurt you physically or mentally.

Day 26

Pretty Girl,

No more excuses!

We all make excuses from time to time when we don't want to do something or we are afraid. You know who you are. You know what you can do. Stop making excuses and do it!

Day 27

You can't CONTROL what people say or DO, but you can CONTROL how it makes you FEEL.
- STARR COBURN

Day 28

Pretty Girl,

Wait, before you change.

Before you change who you are, make sure IT'S something you want to do. Make sure you are changing because it will make you feel better and be a better person that not only adds value to yourself, but to others as well. Don't change who you are to fit who others want you to be. Those who love you will never force you to be something you're not.

Day 29

Pretty Girl,

Ask for Help.

Always ask for help if you don't understand or know how to do something. It doesn't matter what others think. Ask for help if you need it.

It's better to get help and get it right, rather than pretend to know and get it wrong.

Day 30

Pretty Girl,

Be selfless, not selfish.

It's easy to be selfish and always think about yourself, but IT'S better to think about others and help them.
Just think of how amazing the world would be if everyone helped someone else.

Day 31

Pretty Girl,

Always do what's right.

Sometimes, doing the wrong thing seems fun and cool, but it can get you into a lot of trouble, which will cause others to label you as a troublemaker or a bad influence. This can affect how others interact with you. If they feel you are a troublemaker or a person that makes bad choices, they will not want to be around you.

Day 32

Pretty Girl,

Don't be jealous

When you don't like someone because they have or can do something you can't, it makes you angry. It's hard to focus on being the best you, you can be when you are angry. Nobody has anything or can do what you can't. If you work hard toward what you want, one day you may have or can do it. Instead of being Angry, use it as motivation. If they did it You can do it too.

Day 33

It doesn't MATTER what others SEE when they see you. What MATTERS is what YOU SEE when you see YOU.
- STARR COBURN

Day 34

Pretty Girl,

Don't Be so hard on yourself.

Day 35

Pretty Girl,

Follow your dreams.

Dreams are amazing! they help us to visualize places in our mind that our physical body haven't been yet. Though, in order to reach those dreams, you have to work toward them. If you don't put a date on your dream and make it a goal, it will be just another dream.

Day 36

It's IMPOSSIBLE to SUCCESSFULLY move FORWARD if you keep looking BACK.
- **STARR COBURN**

Day 37

Pretty Girl,

You are LOVED.

Day 38

Don't wait for others to shine the spotlight on you. Create your own spotlight.
- STARR COBURN

CHANGE THE WAY YOU SEE YOU

Day 39

Pretty Girl,

You are SPECIAL.

Day 40

Pretty Girl,

Your future is BRIGHT.

Day 41

Pretty Girl,

Don't be like everyone else. Be YOU.

Day 42

Pretty Girl,

Don't be afraid.

Day 43

Pretty Girl,

Your presence is like a beautiful sunshine on a cloudy day.

Day 44

Pretty Girl,

Go for it! you will do great.

Day 45

When you are looking through BROKEN glass, it's hard to see how BEAUTIFUL you are.
- **STARR COBURN**

Day 46

Pretty Girl,

Keep moving forward.

Day 47

Pretty Girl,

They were wrong about you. You are pretty amazing!

Day 48

Pretty Girl,

Don't let anyone steal your smile; it's too precious.

Day 49

Pretty Girl,

Don't change who you are to be who others want you to be.

Day 50

Pretty Girl,

You are wonderfully made. embrace who you are.

Day 51

Pretty Girl,

You are bold, fearless, and confident.

Day 52

Pretty Girl,

Every one doesn't deserve to be in your life.

Day 53

Pretty Girl,

Some people may be happy for you until you start doing better than them.

Day 54

Pretty Girl,

Don't let others define your Beauty.

Day 55

Pretty Girl,

Don't overthink it.

Day 56

Pretty Girl,

Your killing it and looking fabulous!

Day 57

Pretty Girl,

Stay Focused.

Day 58

Pretty Girl,

You don't have to be loud to make noise. Let your presence speak for you.

Day 59

Pretty Girl,

Don't compare yourself to anyone!

Day 60

Pretty Girl,

Be Brave!

Day 61

Pretty Girl,

Aim High!

Day 62

Pretty Girl,

Don't give up on you!

Day 63

Pretty Girl,

You are stronger than you think you are!

Day 64

Pretty Girl,

Believe in yourself because not everyone will.

Day 65

Pretty Girl,

Don't pretend to be great.
BE GREAT!

Day 66

Pretty Girl,

You are a leader. don't let others manipulate you into being a follower.

Day 67

Pretty Girl,

Don't allow anyone to make you feel like You don't belong. You are more than enough.

Day 68

Pretty Girl,

You deserve great things! don't settle for anything short of amazing.

Day 69

Pretty Girl,

You are intelligent, creative, and phenomenal!

Day 70

Pretty Girl,

You don't need permission to be Great, to be unique, to be YOU.

Day 71

Pretty Girl,

Some people may not like being around you because you outshine them, and That's ok. SHINE on! Maybe next time they will bring their sunglasses.

Day 72

Pretty Girl,

Be happy! laugh until your tummy hurts.

Day 73

Pretty Girl,

Don't let other people turn you into something you are not.

Day 74

Pretty Girl,

You are not a failure!

It's ok to fail. After you have failed at something, study to see how you can do it better. Try again.

Day 75

Pretty Girl,

Try again

Just because you don't get it right the first time doesn't mean you can't get it, or it's not meant for you. It may just mean you have to work harder to get it.

Day 76

Persistence is the key to achieving all things great.
- STARR COBURN

Day 77

Pretty Girl,

Change starts with you.

We know the saying, "be the change you want to see". To see change, we must change first. This is true also when it comes to us. If we want to change the way people see and treat us, we must change the way we treat or see ourselves. Lead by example.

Day 78

Pretty Girl,

Dream out loud!

Write down everything you wish to accomplish in your life. It doesn't matter how big or small it is. If you want to travel the world, write it down. Speak it. "I'm going to travel the world." Where are you going to go?

Day 79

FAILURES don't alter your path to success; it tests you to see how bad you want to succeed.
- STARR COBURN

Day 80

Pretty Girl,

Lend a helping hand.

Help those who are in need. If you have knowledge of something that could help someone be better, then share it.

Day 81

Pretty Girl,

Life is full of disappointment, but you are not one.

Day 82

Pretty Girl,

You are remarkable; you can laugh without fear of the future.

Day 83

Pretty Girl,

Change the way you see you!

Take what you have learned and apply it to your life. Once you do, your life will never be the same. You will always see yourself as being amazing because that's what you are!

CHANGE THE WAY YOU SEE YOU

Declare & Decree

I declare and decree
I will do big things
I will be able to pay my bills
I will have excellent credit
I will not be in debt
I will be wise with my money
I will save
I will not go without
I will be wiser as I get older
I will not drop out of school
I will make good grades
I will not be influenced by others to do wrong
I will be a leader
I will not fail and stay down
I will stay in the house I want
I will get the job I want
I will drive the car I want
I will travel the world
I will be whatever I want to be
I will push myself to be better even when it gets hard
I will not settle
I will be rich and not poor
I will accomplish whatever I put my mind to

SPECIAL THANK YOU

Amanda, Deanna, Deanna Hall, Charnyce, Madeline Jackson, CEO of NanaComb Vision, Stella R., Red, Stephanie, Tyisha and a list of other amazing women.

It takes more than a village to help one another. You all are amazing and I appreciate you all for taking time to respond to my post. "What advice would you give the younger you? " Your response helped me put together amazing letters for the Pretty Girl who will read this book.

Stay Connected
Follow Starr Coburn on Facebook

TAKE THE PRETTY GIRL AFFIRMATION ANTHEM CHALLENGE

Rearrange the Pretty Girl Affirmation Anthem (PGAA) the way you like. You can rap or sing it. Do spoken word. Create a skit. Whatever comes to mind? Unleash your inner Pretty Girl. Show the world how amazing you are.
Once you decide how your going to unleash you inner Pretty Girl create a video and post it to your social media site with the following HASHTAGS

#PGAA
#PrettyGirlAffirmationAthem
#PrettyGirlchangethewayyouseeyou
#Letschangetheworldprettygirls
#PrettyGirlBloc

ABOUT THE AUTHOR

Starr Coburn is an outgoing, free spirited individual. She currently resides in Las Vegas, NV but she calls St. Louis, MO and Mississippi home. She is the mother of three amazing boys and wife to a fantastic husband. She has published serval books. She loves people, traveling and writing. Connect with her at www.starr-coburn.com

ANSWERING THE CALL

I hope you enjoyed reading this book as much as I enjoyed writing it. Honestly, I didn't understand why I was writing this book. I didn't feel it was necessary, but after talking to many individuals of various ages and doing a self-evaluation I saw a need that needed to be met. So, I stepped up to the plate and swung. In hopes I would knock it out the park. I'll let you be the judge of that. If this book has helped you, tell someone about it. Tell that young lady who's brokenness is seeping through that she doesn't have to stay that way. Tell her to unleash the Pretty Girl within. Read this book as much as you need. Read the Affirmations and Decrees every day. Create your own and speak them everyday. Our words have power remember that it doesn't matter what others say about you, but what we say about ourselves.

Pretty Girl you are unstoppable. Now that you have Changed the Way you see you, go out and Change the way the world see's you. Don't forget to do the Pretty Girl Affirmation Anthem Challenge and TAG Me.

Additional copies of this book and other books by Starr Coburn can be purchased everywhere books are sold. Order online at www.starrcoburn.com

www.ingramcontent.com/pod-product-compliance
Lightning Source LLC
Chambersburg PA
CBHW071458080526
44587CB00014B/2140